KNOW THYSELF, LOVE THYSELF

A PRACTICAL ROADMAP FOR OPTIMIZING PERFORMANCE, CULTIVATING HEALTHY RELATIONSHIPS, AND CREATING YOUR OWN HEAVEN ON EARTH

KNOW THYSELF, LOVE THYSELF

A PRACTICAL ROADMAP FOR OPTIMIZING PERFORMANCE, CULTIVATING HEALTHY RELATIONSHIPS, AND CREATING YOUR OWN HEAVEN ON EARTH

MIKE WANDLER

ethos collective

KNOW THYSELF, LOVE THYSELF © 2024 by Mike Wandler.
All rights reserved.

Printed in the United States of America

Published by Igniting Souls
PO Box 43, Powell, OH 43065
IgnitingSouls.com

This book contains material protected under international and federal copyright laws and treaties. Any unauthorized reprint or use of this material is prohibited. No part of this book may be reproduced or transmitted in any form or by any means, electronic or mechanical, including photocopying, recording, or by any information storage and retrieval system, without express written permission from the author.

LCCN: 2024904101
Paperback ISBN: 978-1-63680-268-8
Hardcover ISBN: 978-1-63680-269-5
e-book ISBN: 978-1-63680-270-1

Available in paperback, hardcover, e-book, and audiobook.

All Scripture quotations, unless otherwise indicated, are taken from the Holy Bible, New International Version®, NIV®. Copyright © 1973, 1978, 1984 by Biblica, Inc.™ Used by permission of Zondervan. All rights reserved worldwide.

Any Internet addresses (websites, blogs, etc.) and telephone numbers printed in this book are offered as a resource. They are not intended in any way to be or imply an endorsement by Igniting Souls, nor does Igniting Souls vouch for the content of these sites and numbers for the life of this book.

Some names and identifying details may have been changed to protect the privacy of individuals.

Table of Contents

Foreword 1
Note to the Reader 3

PART ONE: Problem

The Hall of Mirrors 7
    How Do You See Life? 11
    Do You Know Yourself? 12
    Do You Love Yourself? 13
    What Happens to Relationships When We Don't
    Know and Love Ourselves? 15
    How Does This Affect Performance? 16

PART TWO: Pyramid

**Chapter One: Strengthening the Muscle
of Your Mind** 21
    Transforming Your Thoughts 22
    My Introduction to Mental Fitness 26
    A Healthy Mind Means Healthy Relationships 28

    What If You Had Healthy Addictions? 31
    Mental Resilience 32

**Chapter Two: Trading Inherited Weaknesses
for Natural Strengths** 37
    Stop Chasing Your Weakness 38
    Don't Share the Suck 41
    Filling the Gaps 45
    Finding Balance 47

**Chapter Three: Setting Yourself Up for Success:
Defining Your Mission, Vision, and Values** 50
    Identifying Your Values 51
    Crafting a Compelling Vision 55
    Forging a Mountain-Moving Mission 56
    Bigger Than You Might Imagine 58

**Chapter Four: Accomplishing More in Less Time:
The Art of Flow** 59
    Making the Pyramid Work for You 61
    Getting Flow to Work for You 64
    Don't Make it Too Easy 65
    We Need Great Conductors 66

PART THREE: Practice

Chapter Five: Staying On Top 73
    The Most Valuable Type of Energy 75
    Setting High Expectations 77
    Quality of Life vs. Quantity of Life 79
    Crafting Your Own Heaven on Earth 81

Endnotes 85
About the Author 89

Foreword

The moment I heard Mike Wandler speak in a Strategic Coach® workshop, I said to myself, "I want to get to know more about this guy and his business."

First off, I was deeply impressed with his value proposition statement, "We design, manufacture, and maintain the biggest machines on the earth." Secondly, I was also impressed with the way he viewed productivity, team management, and energy efficiency. With a closer look, I discovered he was doing something unique and different, because his results were unique and different.

The truth is we live in a fast-paced, complex, and ever-changing world. This world brings with it a plethora of difficult questions and challenges on a daily basis.

- How do we cope with the stress, pressure, and uncertainty?

Foreword

- How do we achieve our goals and fulfill our potential?
- How do we create meaningful and lasting relationships with ourselves and others?
- How do we find happiness and peace in the midst of chaos and turmoil?

We're left asking a simple yet profound question: Is it possible to possess soul-deep fortitude that can truly prepare you for any difficulty?

Mike Wandler says yes. And he shows us how in his inspiring and practical book, *Know Thyself, Love Thyself*. Drawing from his own memory of a life-threatening panic attack, Mike shares his journey of self-discovery and self-love, and how it transformed his life, his family, and his business. He reveals the secrets of his own exponential growth, and how he uses those to create a culture of trust, collaboration, and excellence.

Know Thyself, Love Thyself is more than just a book. It is a roadmap for anyone who wants to unlock their inner power, unleash their creativity, and live with passion and purpose. It is a gift for anyone who wants to know themselves better, love themselves more, and share their light with the world.

I have had the privilege of knowing Mike for several years, and I can attest to his authenticity, integrity, and generosity. He is a visionary leader, a compassionate mentor, and a loyal friend. He is someone who walks his talk and inspires others to do the same. He is someone who has been tried by fire and has learned through it all both to know himself and love himself.

Let Mike be your guide through your own trials, and rely on his experience to help you find a sustainable source of internal energy through self-discovery.

—Dr. Kary Oberbrunner, CEO of Igniting Souls, *Wall Street Journal* and *USA Today* Bestselling Author

Note to the Reader

L&H Industrial manufactures parts for the biggest machines on earth. It's not the kind of place you'd normally find folks talking about mental fitness or knowing themselves. In fact, this shop in Wyoming full of welders, mechanics, and engineers might be the last spot you'd expect to find people focusing on mental fitness and flow.

However, L&H is also in the energy business. I'm constantly on the lookout for innovative, competitive energy sources. Safe, clean, renewable energy is even more necessary in the lives of human beings. The energy produced by humans and animals is base-level energy. Everything we more traditionally call energy is a tool for humans to use. I find the energy produced by men and women tremendously fascinating. When this energy is maximized, it's a gold mine. Sadly, humans expend unnecessary effort each day on self-preservation and worry.

Note to the Reader

When my wife and I met Travis Ramsey, we began to be excited about the amount of energy and joy his mental fitness coaching could create. We discovered when each member of our family and our team had access to his remarkable skills, they could tackle any crisis, learn to know and love themselves, and when ready, move into high-performance mode and compound their productivity using less energy. Even better, they could create a bit of utopia right in their own world.

Though we saw the potential, we had no idea the enormous transformation Travis would bring. We've experienced increased safety awareness, a higher level of productivity and quality, and employees' lives saved. No one could have convinced me how desperately we needed someone like him ten years ago.

Better yet, this same structure works in other relationships just as easily as it does in the workplace. Since we added a mental fitness coach to the L&H team, we've seen marriages saved and suicides averted. The entire transformative process made such a major difference that I felt compelled to share.

So many people put performance in one category and love in another; however, we've discovered when you love yourself, what you do, and those you work with, performance increases exponentially. I'm truly excited to share with the world our Performance Pyramid. We use it to demonstrate the steps necessary to find that place where we can find renewed energy. It illustrates the recipe for optimized performance, extraordinary mental fitness, healthy relationships, and a little taste of Heaven here on Earth.

PART ONE
Problem

The Hall of Mirrors

Man can alter his life by altering his thinking.
—William James

I don't look or sound like the kind of guy you would expect to have anxiety issues. A business owner and gearhead, my deep voice and size probably intimidate folks. To top it off, I'd never had any kind of anxiety problems. So, no one was more surprised than me when a couple of panic attacks while scuba diving immobilized me.

I had been diving for years when the first attack hit. My wife, Jerri, and I were diving in Cuba. Sketchy equipment and guides probably should have kept me from taking the excursion, but we got in the boat and made our way out to sea with twenty others despite the fact high waves rocked the craft.

The Hall of Mirrors

The guides dropped anchor as the bow lifted eight feet before it crashed into the rough water. Still, twenty men and women in diving gear made their way to the front of the boat. We would all descend the anchor line to get to the calmer waters beneath the surface.

Jerri and I jumped in to wait our turn to follow the chain to the bottom; however, I lost it. I felt like someone was sitting on my chest. I gasped for air, but nothing helped my straining lungs. Everyone else started yelling in panic while Jerri helped me to the back of the boat. Even with her help, I could barely get up the ladder.

When I finally made it to the deck, I spent the next half hour embarrassed, ashamed, and confused. *What the hell just happened?* Jerri and the captain worried I was having a heart attack. I sat and recovered while the other divers finished their expedition.

I spent the time trying to figure out why my body reacted to the water. *Was I worried about Jerri in the turbulent sea?* It couldn't have been a fear of losing control. I had been deep under the water at least fifty times before with no issues.

I finally just moved on. It didn't really matter what caused it, right? Everything returned to normal until my friend Demir Mollaoglu from Istanbul took me out on the Mediterranean. His captain, a professional dive master, transferred to a dinghy with Demir and me. His first mate dropped us in the middle of the water and headed back to the boat. The seas were rough, but we would dive deep and work our way back to the boat.

The moment I hit the water, the same overwhelming sense of panic overwhelmed me. Luckily, Demir's captain, Denniz Oludeniz, was a pro. He immediately noticed something was wrong. He tried everything to talk me down, but I couldn't get past the panic. The way it paralyzed me made me sure this would be my last underwater adventure. Dennis dropped my weights, aired up my buoyancy control device (BCD), and told me to swim to a nearby boulder-laden island with waves crashing against it while he went back for Demir.

The few hundred yards seemed like forever. With a pounding heart and energy depleted, I headed toward the treacherous landing. I don't remember much except paddling toward the island until Demir and Denniz pulled me onto a boulder to get me out of harm's way. They saved my life, and we waited for the first mate and my cousin, Paul Wandler, to come looking for us. It took him an hour to realize we had abandoned the dive. I spent the time recovering, feeling embarrassed and confused. Like the others, Paul, who is also an L&H quality director, wondered and worried about what happened.

I obviously survived, but the ordeals threw me. I had never been irrationally afraid of anything before. It just didn't make sense. If I wanted to dive, I had to figure out what triggered the fear. That's when I met Travis Ramsey. Travis was a leader at 40 Years of Zen, a neurofeedback retreat I booked for Jerri, my Sister Laura, and me.

During the retreat, one of the traumatic experiences that my sister dealt with was an incident at a hotel pool in North Dakota. Laura was about eight when the family traveled to visit my grandparents. My sister wasn't a strong swimmer yet, but Mom put three-year-old me on her shoulders in the shallow end while she went back to the room for a minute. My five-year-old brother Jeff played in the water nearby.

With all the splashing and laughing, no one noticed when Laura started bouncing too close to the deep end. When her feet didn't quite touch, she had to get me off her shoulders to keep from drowning.

Laura told us my brother Jeff jumped in and pulled me to safety. Though I nearly drowned, I didn't remember any of it until she shared the story of her childhood traumatic event. Then in a flash, the memory rushed back, and I realized the rough waters of a hotel pool and nearly drowning at three caused my unprovoked hysteria. This terrifying moment had lived buried, completely insignificant, for thirty-five years, deep within my psyche until I decided to dive into rough waters.

Travis took me on a journey toward learning how to respond when I feel myself getting amped up. He taught me how to reset my brain when I felt anxiety and how to let go of whatever attempted to hold me captive in the moment.

However, before I could transform my thinking, I had to know myself. The bit of seemingly irrelevant information my sister shared made all the difference in setting me free. I had to understand the root before I could stop the debilitating attacks,

Everything I learned from Travis set me on a path to knowing myself better. He taught me to let go of trauma from my past—first one, then the next, and the next. It was liberating and empowering.

Julia Waller, the Strategic Coach® Unique Ability® guru, also added to my transformation. She took me to a whole new level of understanding my unique abilities and helped me see the value in spending as much time as possible working in them. Their lessons made me want to help others discover the freedom I found in discovering the depths of my soul. I started to realize the better I know myself, the more I love myself, and the richer my life becomes. The average person doesn't even realize Heaven on Earth is possible. I didn't until I met Travis and Julia.

How Do You See Life?

Overwhelming—that's how most people describe their lives. Every aspect contains worries. We try to focus on something other than the problems, but we can't see past the trouble. The struggle is real.

Many blame a lack of physical needs on the state of their thoughts and feelings; however, I've seen smiling families enjoying life in Africa who have nothing but a sad roof over their heads and a meal or two a day. It's as if they don't have a worry in the world. Obviously, our feelings of shame, guilt, anxiety, and despair go beyond material things.

Others feel like their DNA controls much of their life. Studies refute this argument. In his book *Longevity*, Peter Diamandis tells us heredity accounts for only seven percent of our heritage. Oxford University reports our DNA is responsible for a little over eight percent.

One last scapegoat people use to predict their future is the victim-of-our-environment excuse. Many ultra-successful celebrities cause us to question this theory. Steelers running back Najee Harris spent time in several homeless shelters with his mother and siblings as a child. Bengals receiver Terrell Owens has a similar story. Abandoned by his father, his mother worked tirelessly to put food on the table. Country legends Dolly Parton and Loretta Lynn both endured extreme poverty.

My own history proves the environment theory is just an excuse. My paternal grandmother died when my dad, Leon Wandler, was just five. His father abandoned the children, carousing in drunkenness instead of caring for his two daughters and three sons. My father and his siblings barely survived. They ended up in an orphanage, raised by hard-nosed, ill-tempered nuns. Despite their difficult childhood, most of the Wandler children used this experience as a catalyst to success. The celebrities and my aunts and uncles all saw life as something to be conquered rather than a hindrance with power to hold them back.

I feel bad for the number of people who feel like external forces have limited their finances and time. We live in an era of immense freedom. Still, many feel hemmed in. I've seen people who appear to have it all—a great job, a wonderful family, and more—live in a world of negativity and criticism. They push themselves to do more and be more. They look for the next big thing to bring success, and when it comes, it doesn't satisfy.

Do You Know Yourself?

Socrates said, "To know thyself is the beginning of wisdom." Unfortunately, few truly know their inner selves. They don't feel passionate about anything, or if they do, they've inherited the value from someone else. They feel out of sync with themselves, so the rest of the world seems to be passing them by.

Even before television and social media, people tried to emulate others. Today, with the bombardment of advertising trying to convince us what it means to be beautiful, successful, and happy, figuring out who you are is even more difficult.

With teens, the symptoms are more obvious. These young people worry about what their peers will think. They get caught up in how they look, and finding their rank on the social ladder consumes them. Their attempts to fit in steal any sense of identity.

As adults, we would like to think we've outgrown the lack of self-confidence that sent us chasing after what the crowd thought; however, if we're honest, most of us hide our true selves in the shadows, hoping no one will notice. We've allowed our vibrations, our thoughts and feelings, to turn to humiliation, blame, despair, and regret, and we've done it for so long that life looks bleak, and we don't know who we are anymore.

Unfortunately, when we don't know ourselves, we feel inadequate. This lack of knowing who we are leads to those feelings of being overwhelmed, inadequate, and lost. And those internal thoughts eventually spew themselves out in words and actions, spraying the junk those feelings produce all over anyone close to us.

> What you see in other people is a reflection of yourself. A person of goodness sees goodness in others, and a person of evil sees evil in others. – Omar Suleiman

Omar Suleiman said, "What you see in other people is a reflection of yourself. A person of goodness sees goodness in others, and a person of evil sees evil in others." It's called mirroring.[1] Think about the trait in your child that sticks out to you the most. If you're honest, you'll admit they learned it from you. It could be good or bad; however, if the trait is one you don't like in yourself, it becomes magnified because mirroring lets us see the unwelcome trait above all others.

Do You Love Yourself?

For every person who doesn't know themselves is a person who doesn't like themselves. Those same advertisements that make you question who you are also invade your brain with the message you aren't enough. They subliminally tell us we can't like ourselves because we fall short on many levels.

Nearly every major religion has an adage similar to the commands Jesus gave his disciples, "Do to others as you would have them do unto you" (Matthew 7:12) and "Love your neighbor as yourself" (Matthew 22:39). I can't help but

The Hall of Mirrors

wonder if the reason the world is in such a state is because most people don't live those words. What if bullies and gang members are loving their neighbors just as much as they love themselves? How many of them don't love themselves because they don't have anything bigger to believe in? If our capacity to share love is directly related to the way we feel about ourselves, something needs to change.

> **Insecurity stems from concentrating our focus on protecting ourselves from being hurt or embarrassed.**

Most people who spend their energy being nasty are mirroring their love for themselves. They see their reflection in others and project their self-loathing on the poor souls who inadvertently point out their worst traits. Sadly, when we don't love ourselves, we don't even recognize the ugliness we're spreading.

Many mistakenly believe every person who looks self-confident loves themselves. Those same folks often think self-confidence is the same as arrogance. Self-loathers criticize and berate themselves thinking it's an admirable quality. This attitude isn't any better than arrogance. Self-deprecation, like arrogance, especially when it spills over into narcissistic behavior, is a cover for insecurity.

Insecurity stems from concentrating our focus on protecting ourselves from being hurt or embarrassed. We can't put energy into loving others because every ounce goes into self-preservation.[2] The consequences of this lack of love include unhealthy addictions, fear, and hostility. People who don't love themselves see themselves as worthless and feel unbalanced.

The way we view ourselves falls on a long continuum ranging from "I love myself" at its highest point to "I can't even look at myself in the mirror" at its lowest. Managers whose self-love falls on the lower third of the spectrum feel a need to belittle their team. Abusive parents treat their children badly because they don't like their reflection. But how do we heal these damaged connections?

What Happens to Relationships When We Don't Know and Love Ourselves?

Everyone wants unshakeable relationships, but interacting with others is difficult. Often, misunderstandings and differences lead to frustration. Perhaps you have been in a relationship turned nightmare. My wife and I were each twice divorced when we met over twenty years ago. Allowing harmful associations to develop and staying in them for extended periods is a symptom of not knowing and loving yourself.

Even the best of relationships have a myriad of dynamics. Friendship, marriage, dating, living together, child/parent, coworkers, and more—they all come with their own nuances and problems. But a critical inner dialogue compounds the problems.

When people don't know and love themselves, it's difficult to develop deep connections. Stress escalates when you live in fear of losing the people you care about. Will my spouse leave? Will our children go to college and not come back? Without the confidence that comes from knowing and loving oneself, one of two things happens. Either people hold on so tightly their greatest fear becomes reality, or they won't set boundaries and find themselves taken advantage of or abused. In the absence of self-knowledge and self-love, subtle differences and lack of accountability turn into explosive situations.

To make matters worse, we tend to attract people who are most like us. If we're negative and self-critical, that's the kind of tribe we draw. Every conversation becomes draining to the soul because no one brings light into the relationship. And unfortunately, when we do occasionally find someone who will feed positivity into our lives, if we continually invite them to our pity parties and never walk with them in their joy, the relationship won't be sustainable.

In the workplace, mirroring causes us to judge our coworkers according to our faults and failures. Because we don't know ourselves, rather than striving to do our best and helping others on our team be their best, we constantly compare ourselves and compete with those we work next to.

Because we see others through the light of mirroring, every view we have of them is an angle of comparison. It's like we're at a circus, walking through the hall of mirrors. All we see are distorted, mangled images. We never truly know the people we care about or work with because we don't know ourselves.

How Does This Affect Performance?

People who don't know who they are and don't love themselves get stuck. I've seen it over and over again. We can tell when someone is struggling with personal relationships because they become distracted, unsafe, and unproductive. They stand, locked in time, waiting for everything around them to fall into place. With relationships in turmoil, they can't focus on the job. The guilt and shame they feel for how they treated a spouse or children or how they were treated robs them of their ability to reach their full potential.

When someone is struggling with personal relationships, they become distracted, unsafe, and unproductive.

Know Thyself, Love Thyself

It's difficult to do your best work when you feel as though life is out of control and external forces have the upper hand. Additionally, living in the negative leads to serious health problems. Besides being harmful to relationships, damaging our self-esteem, and bringing anxiety and depression, those pessimistic thoughts can lead to high blood pressure and reduce the ability to fight illness.[3] Negativity has the potential to take over our lives if we give it permission.

Because L&H Industrial has intentionally built our Pyramid with the priority and foundation of consistently focusing on keeping our team mentally fit, we've seen incredible professional gains. The beauty of reaching the top of the pyramid is when you're there, you're untouchable. And when each member of the tribe is in flow, the combined force creates an organizational flow of excellence.

With each person working in their natural strengths toward one common goal, we actually create energy rather than deplete it. The entire process becomes so natural, you don't think about it. In fact, we rarely even realize our productivity is two to five times the rest of the industry until customers begin to experience it and mention the differences.

So few realize the disservice they do to themselves and those around them by not learning to know and love themselves. They open themselves to a world of endless problems with no way out. You might call it Hell on Earth.

Fewer understand the connection between performance and love. However, when we combine the two, we create exponential power. Performance isn't sustainable if you don't love what you're doing and love those you're working with.

Everything becomes possible when you become mentally fit. So walk with me for a bit. Let me take you up the Performance Pyramid so you can discover how to create your own slice of Heaven on Earth.

PART TWO
Pyramid

CHAPTER ONE

Strengthening the Muscle of Your Mind

Your mind is the strongest and most valuable muscle you can grow in the gym.

—Greg Plitt

I have good news and bad news.

The bad news is our lives are exactly what we've set them up to be. People push back when I say that. Most who live in misery tell me, "I certainly wouldn't have set up this life." Unfortunately, it's a truth we can't escape.

But the good news is by accepting this reality, you have the capability to change it. You're not too old, and you're not too young. It doesn't matter what your bank account says or what job you're currently working. American philosopher and psychologist William James said, "If you can change your mind, you can change your life." Embracing the fact you get to choose whether you live in misery or joy has more potential and power than you can imagine, and the transformation begins when you believe in your ability to choose.

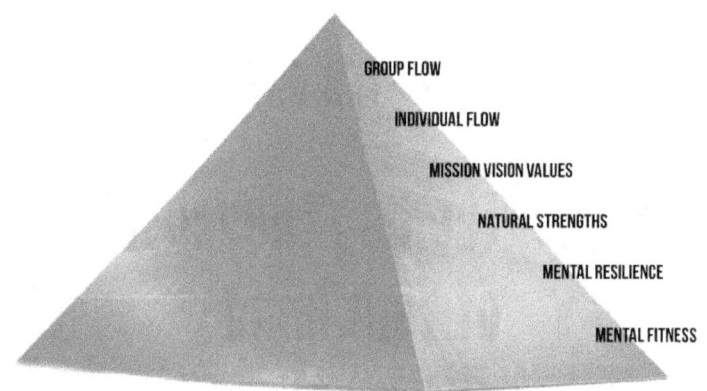

The Performance Pyramid has become a staple in the L&H Industrial business model. Our tribe has proven that by taking the steps on this figure, we can reach the top of the mountain—a state of flow and a place where every action we take feels natural and uncomplicated. Our team has demonstrated it is truly possible to create your own Heaven on Earth, and it all begins with strengthening your mind.

Transforming Your Thoughts

It's fascinating how much our perception of life writes the narrative for and controls the way we deal with individual circumstances. Three children, all raised by the same parents, take in things from completely different points of view. One will see the parents as evil and overbearing, while the other two describe those same parents as loving and understanding.

What one views as traumatic, another shrugs off as a simple part of life. No one is right or wrong. It's not a matter of who is correct. It boils down to how each person viewed the different situations and the way their brains processed them.

> **All that we are arises with our thoughts. With our thoughts, we make the world. – Buddha**

To be mentally fit, we have to return to our past and face some of those traumatic events and things that formed our perceptions, like my near drowning. By revisiting them, we can own them and take control of the way they feed our emotions.

Andrew Carnegie, David Schwartz, Confucious, Buddha, and others all said some form of the phrase, "You are what you think." Henry Ford's actual words were, "Whether you think you can or can't, you're correct." Your mind holds magnificent power. Making certain its power always works to your advantage means becoming mentally fit.

Mental fitness is the foundation for knowing and loving yourself, and the key to strengthening your mind is found in transforming your thoughts.

One of the most fantastic discoveries of the twentieth century was found in the brain. Prior to the early 1900s, scientists believed the brain could not be changed. They thought the mind you were born with was the mind you had your entire life. However, in 1948, Jerry Konorski observed changes in the neuron structure of the brain.[4]

Since then, huge advancements in research have given psychologists and counselors the tools necessary to help humans renew their minds. This means people who've suffered from strokes can be rehabilitated, and memory can be enhanced. It also means we have the power to rewire our brains.

Your brain has approximately 100 billion neurons sending messages to every part of your body with the ability to develop new neural pathways and prune old ones. By feeding our brain positive messages, we have the power to strengthen the circuits giving us positive thoughts. Meanwhile, as we decrease the amount of negativity we allow to inhabit our brain, we reduce the synaptic connections sending our brain down those unpleasant rabbit holes.[5][6]

Wouldn't you love to exude positivity and demonstrate a deep-seated love for yourself? Anyone can journey down the road of neuroplastic transformation. Regardless of whether you choose to do it on your own or find a mental fitness trainer, the process takes commitment and a conscious choice to be different.

Workout gurus say it in a variety of ways, but all agree physical fitness begins in the kitchen. They have as many diets as they have ways to phrase it. In the same way, scientists have determined many foods and supplements to aid in memory and brain building. And while your diet will help in your mind makeover, feeding the brain goes way beyond your refrigerator.

Doctors and weight loss programs frown on mindless eating, but even worse is what we feed our brains mindlessly. Every second of every day, our brains receive eleven million bits of information.[7] Every sensory organ sends it messages, and the biggest culprits of damaging information are our eyes and ears.

Movies, music, books, social media, television, news, conversations, and more can poorly or positively impact our neurons. Earl Nightengale said, "The mind, like the land, will return what you plant, but it doesn't care what you plant." If we aren't intentional about what we allow to filter through those senses and plant in our minds, it's as if we're snacking in front of the television in the middle of our weight loss plan.

One person on our team has given up watching the news. She's found this bombardment of negativity wasn't good for her mental fitness. Others have passed on social media because they realize photos of vacations make them feel cheated because they haven't been able to sit on the beach. Comparing their life to others trips up their thinking, so they've chosen to remove the feeder of comparisons.

Mirroring can actually work in our favor as we attempt to transform our thoughts. If we're aware of the fact we may be projecting our own traits onto others, we can learn from what we see. When another person continually acts in a way that drives us crazy, we need to ask, "Am I really seeing myself magnified?" or "Do I act like that?"

If it seems as if everyone else in the world is negative or mean, perhaps you should listen to yourself or review your own point of view.

> If it seems as if everyone else in the world is negative or mean, perhaps you should listen to yourself or review your own point of view.

Though sometimes complete opposites stand out to us, if we pause for a moment and reflect on our own thoughts when we run into excessive negativity, what we learn can help us grow and mature.[8]

As I've developed mental fitness, I've begun to look at people differently. I now know nasty people are really talking to themselves. Unfortunately, their self-talk ends up spraying out on anyone nearby. Listen to what they say. The more you understand yourself, the more you'll hear their self-criticism. They see themselves in the person next to them, and they don't like it. They're rejecting themselves through that other person.

My Introduction to Mental Fitness

Our minds are fascinating things. Mine had developed a mechanism to protect the three-year-old me from the memory of the pool incident. Our brains lock away stuff they don't think we can handle. Those memories of my pool mishap couldn't have chosen a worse time to surface and squirt out, but my brain couldn't contain them anymore. Stress will often force the memories up and out. In my case, it was when I put myself into a similar situation without even realizing it.

There in the water, I became an observer of my life. Paralyzed by a fear I couldn't explain, participation became impossible. Though I didn't remember being under the water when I was three, the dive brought back every ounce of anxiety and stress I felt as a toddler. Feelings I didn't understand and couldn't control dictated my reality at that moment.

Working with Travis, I went back to that summer day at the pool. I inserted myself into that place and time and gave myself permission to feel the emotions that accompanied my experience. I looked at who was to blame and forgave them. Still, the fear the trauma caused remained. Travis told me to go back to the meditation and consider the worst that could have happened. That did it! I realized the worst that could have happened is I could have died! Only one thing seemed worse than death—the fear and anxiety of dying.

The realization allowed me to release all my anxiety over the incident. I could feel it start to melt away. We revisited the event a few more times until there was no emotion left around it. Without the energy of anxiety and stress, the event had no more power. However, I learned I had additional situations from my past shrouded in emotional energy. Some I possessed full memory of, but I had no idea they had a bit of trauma connected to them.

Some therapists use breakthrough therapies involving ketamine, MDMA, or classic psychedelic compounds such as mushrooms to help people walk through the doors of those painful experiences. These compounds help push people past those things their minds try to protect them from. When people use mushrooms and say they had a bad trip, it means the drug took them through a door they weren't ready to open. Their minds naturally wanted to shelter them from the memories they found there.

Fortunately, you can walk through most doors without the aid of drugs. I highly recommend learning these skills and clearing out everything possible through meditation and resets. Save the ketamine for the ones you can't overcome, and make sure you have a master guide who can provide the right set and setting.

Knocking down walls of mental protection means getting to know yourself better. I had to get in tune with my feelings and actions. I learned I need to pay attention each time my shoulders tense or I get distracted. Something triggers those reactions. I need to dig until I figure it out.

We're all like pressure cookers, and some of us have more past events heating up the pot than others. Circumstances constantly cause pressure to build in our lives. And regardless of how long it takes, like the pressure cooker, what's inside will eventually have to be released. We can learn a process to control the release, or we can walk around oblivious until it explodes and burns everyone around us.

By taking time to sit and meditate or pray, I allow myself to go back to the spot causing the tension. Travis taught me to unpack the situation, accurately identify the people who caused the tension, and pinpoint as many of the triggers as possible. Recognizing every aspect allows me to let go and reset my mind. The recognition doesn't change the reality of the event; however, it robs the memory of its power. Like my underwater experience, we usually don't realize we have triggers until we get into the middle of a door-opening situation.

I had to learn to recognize what made me tense and stole my attention. With each past event that I took time to analyze, I started to appreciate myself more. Getting to know myself better allowed Travis to teach me reset techniques that gave me peace. I haven't yet tried to dive again; however, I'm confident when I do, I will be able to deal with the anxiety my past caused.

A Healthy Mind Means Healthy Relationships

Relationships have a huge impact on our mental fitness. For the most part, we need other people. Unfortunately, dealing with other humans isn't always easy. Humans love it when everything conforms to the familiar—which life seldom does. When we aren't mentally fit, we'll find ourselves in the middle of misunderstandings. Connecting with others authentically can be nearly impossible until we know and truly love ourselves. And after we know and love ourselves, we begin to better know and love others.

If we're transforming our thoughts, we're committing to working on relationships as well. And the first relationship you have to work on is the one you have with yourself. Love recognizes and accepts. It embraces individual natures and natural strengths. Do you treat yourself with love, patience, and kindness? Because that's what love does. If you find yourself constantly treating others badly, you should look at how you feel about yourself, as the mirroring effect often reveals our self-love or loathing.

When we learn to love ourselves, we evaluate the connections we currently have to see which of the people in our lives truly want us to be our best selves. We need the strongest connections to be those people we truly trust. Sometimes this is difficult to discern because we've been betrayed so often we're afraid to trust anyone. Nevertheless, if you look deep, you'll find one or two people who have your back no matter what. And if you don't, then it's time to consider what you're feeding into the relationship.

Love is the recognition and acceptance of one's own and others' true selves. It allows us to embrace individual natures and unique abilities. Love fosters collaboration rather than seeking change, and actively gathers and retains a tribe that aligns with one's personal and professional mission, vision, and values.

> **Love is the recognition and acceptance of one's own and others' true selves.**

Countless studies have been conducted on the role of relationships in people who seem to be thriving emotionally and mentally. One such study showed that positive relationships enable us to pursue bigger opportunities. The mindset of our friends and family spills onto us. Often if they think we can handle a new career or a challenging endeavor, we do too.

Healthy relationships also allow us to more easily find our purpose and meaning in life. We have a desire to learn, grow, and explore. This allows us to expand our minds and focus on the positive. Plus, these connections keep our physical bodies healthier.[9]

On the other hand, we have to be on the lookout for harmful relationships. We may need to break ties with some people or limit our exposure to people in our family who damage our mental fitness. Often, the actions are completely unintentional; however, overprotective partners, acquaintances who like to pass out blame, and parents who feel a need to control can hinder our mental growth.

Maintaining healthy relationships means we give back at least as much as we get. We can't keep a tally board; it's not about being even. At the same time, if people continually feed into us and we never give back, we can't call the relationship healthy. When we don't agree with someone, we have to decide how important it is to be right in that moment. Will being right or letting it go make the relationship stronger?

These two-way healthy connections help us with our mental fitness because the more we support others, the more we realize our importance. We feel better about ourselves when we know we've helped someone else through their difficult moments.

Another relationship I encourage you to pursue is a connection to something greater than yourself. Alcoholics Anonymous calls it their higher power, Masons label it the Grand Architect of the Universe, and Jews and Christians pray to God. I am not at all religious; however, I am spiritual, and I believe being connected to something greater brings purpose into our lives. This spirituality helps us navigate life's journey with trust and grace and has the potential to make us better human beings. The faith accompanying spirituality bleeds over into believing in yourself. It allows you to develop a much clearer picture of who you are.

There's a difference between faith and religion. Faith has its roots in the spiritual. It believes in something bigger and better and uses belief to inspire hope. Religion focuses on rituals and rules. It counts on fear to control, manipulate, and keep people within its boundaries. Don't let a minority of extremists who have done horrendous things in the name of some religion rob you of this cornerstone to mental fitness.

What If You Had Healthy Addictions?

Humans are addictive by nature. To think you'll remove all addictions from your life is unrealistic. You can, however, use your mind transformation to secure addictions that serve you. Our brain and biology are excellent at giving us a euphoric feeling. You can see it in children. They laugh and expend more energy than adults can imagine.

But that utopian feeling doesn't have to end with childhood. We have the potential to reach what Steven Kotler calls Cloud Nine. A healthy addiction feeds that natural euphoria and allows it to grow. It brings peace and makes you a better you. Exercise can be a healthy addiction. The dopamine and endorphins we release during physical activity give us energy. Music works in a similar way; however, a music addiction can help relieve anxiety, stress, and depression.

Even these healthy addictions can be damaging if we take them too far. Like the more well-known unhealthy addictions—drugs, alcohol, gambling, cigarettes, caffeine, and sugar—they can separate us from family and friends or take away from the time we should be spending at work. Fortunately, healthy addictions and their natural chemical releases have less chance of becoming dangerous.

The excessive amounts of chemicals these addictions produce take us to a place of euphoria. However, when the chemicals come from external sources, and we allow them to create a utopian state for an extended period of time, our internal chemical supplies stop producing. Our brain figures if we don't need it, it's not going to do the work. For a while, we'll get a fake version of the high, but eventually, euphoria becomes impossible. The addiction creates a numbing instead of a utopia. We've all seen the consequences of these painful addictions.

It's nearly impossible to get rid of unhealthy addictions. It's much easier to replace an unhealthy addiction with a healthy one rather than simply discard the old one. In addition to exercise and music, meditation can reduce stress and improve focus, reading makes us more empathetic and improves health, journaling can enhance our problem-solving skills, and volunteering gives us new connections.[10] Each of these can replace unhealthy addictions and increase our mental fitness.

Addictions can ruin our mental fitness. It's vital to be sure that we maintain a balance of moderation even with the most healthy of addictions. It's also important to incorporate these health addictions because they help strengthen our minds and increase our capacity to bounce back when life strikes.

Mental Resilience

You might be thinking, "All I have to do is stay away from people, and I'll be fine." But would you really be living? Alec Vetter was known as "The Bubble Boy." Born in 1971, he was placed in a completely sterile environment within twenty seconds of his birth. The twelve years he lived were as pleasant as possible thanks to help from NASA, but he never felt a touch and had limited contact with people. If he had stepped outside his bubble or his spacesuit for even a few seconds, he would have experienced pain and death.

Likewise, we can't truly experience life in seclusion. Without developing mental resilience, one step out of a people-free environment, and we get knocked over.

In the world of bodybuilders, coaches say, "Strength is the ability to exert force, and resilience is the ability to withstand and absorb force." Fighters have to learn how to absorb punches. If a strong man can't bounce back quickly from an injury, those muscles he spent weeks developing will quickly deteriorate. The best weightlifters understand the need to strengthen even the small underlying muscles to ensure a quick recovery when trauma occurs.[11]

Our minds work the same way. In addition to being mentally fit, we need to develop mental resilience. We begin by asking, "What kinds of things can tip me over?"

Death, divorce, and depression all have the potential to knock us over. Even some celebratory moments can catch us off guard. Children moving out of the house or the end of a huge project can cause some people to feel lost because it marks a transition from familiar to something new. Many things in life will push you past your limits. Mental resilience is the ability to bounce back.

Stop and consider things others have said that derailed you. How long did it take you to recover? How well do you take constructive criticism? Some folks personalize every word to the point it ruins their day or week. Do you get thrown off by a mere look or an innocent remark? If so, you probably need to build your mental resilience. Mental fragility has ruined relationships and marriages because one or both parties couldn't recover from a misspoken word or a hurtful mistake.

Mental fitness does not mean the ugliness and doubt will stop. People will still come at us. Often, they won't mean to knock us over, but every now and then, the attack will be intentional. Either way, the fact is we will occasionally be caught off guard by someone else's actions. Failure can hit us the same way. When we think we've completed the project perfectly, but the manager asks us to completely rework it, the feeling of incompetence can take the wind out of our sails. Nelson Mandela once said, "Do not judge me by my success, judge me by how many times I fell down and got back up again." Mental resilience gives us the power to endure the occasional but inevitable feelings of inadequacy.

It's important to recognize the difference between Mental Resilience and Mental Fragility. Understanding the nuances can help us identify triggers that attempt to push us over the edge. Recognizing those things that spark our emotions or cause tension can help us take control and respond appropriately.

> **Do not judge me by my success, judge me by how many times I fell down and got back up again.**
> –Nelson Mandela

What do you do when someone gives you a look or speaks a hurtful word? Are you unmoved or undone, unbothered or triggered? Do you step toward or away from uncomfortable situations? Do you depend on relationships to bring you happiness, or can you love yourself independently? How do you react to drama? Do you own it or allow the dramatic people to keep it for themselves? What about crisis and death? Can you persevere, or will you perish? Can you survive and thrive, or will you be fearful and flee?

EVENT	Mental Resiliency	Mental Fragility
Look	I'm unmoved	I'm undone
Word	I'm unbothered	I'm triggered
Situation	Step Toward	Step Away
Relationship	Independent	Dependent
Drama	It's theirs	It's mine
Crisis	I will persevere	I will perish
Death	I will survive and thrive	I will fear and flee

Unfortunately, because pain builds inside people who don't know and love themselves, we're forced to sometimes deal with those lower levels of vibration—thoughts and emotions that lead to guilt, shame, apathy, and grief. Some religions resort to manipulating those lower vibrations. Often, they think they can help people become better; however, their tactics are mean. Trying to change someone, even if it is in their best interest, using guilt to motivate or control is wrong. Mental fitness allows us to recognize these traps, and mental resilience keeps us from taking ownership of the guilt these individuals and organizations try to dish out.

Those healthy relationships I mentioned earlier play a pivotal part in mental resilience. Often, when we go through difficulties, we withdraw rather than reach out. However, supportive family and friends are what we need to help pick us up when we fall.

We shouldn't seek out people who add to our pity party. Instead, look for connections who listen well and offer advice when needed but are willing to sit with you quietly if that's what the current situation needs. These kinds of relationships strengthen our psychological well-being. They remind us to have faith in humans when it's another human who pushed us over.

Mental resilience will become useful as you age as well. People who've worked in the same job for decades feel as though they've lost themselves when something happens to end their employment. A few want to work until they die; however, the physical exertion required for the job forces them into retirement. The average person needs to be mentally prepared for career changes. Layoffs, shutdowns, and surgeries all necessitate moves in careers. Let's face it. Football players can't keep taking tackles when they're seventy. Learning mental resilience helps us bounce back from life changes. It keeps us from feeling useless and can literally keep us young.

Thanks to everything I've learned about mental fitness and resilience, I choose to let love, peace, joy, and enlightenment flow through me. I want respect and an incredible sense of transcendence to shape my existence. This is the highest level of vibration, and it allows us to develop better relationships and withstand those moments trying to knock us over.

We need mental fitness and mental resilience to keep us out of crisis. They boost our immune system so we can heal from nasty illnesses. These are the building blocks for your Heaven on Earth.

Without mental fitness, you're building your pyramid on a house of cards. You could keep going, but it will eventually all fall apart. After you've built this strong foundation, you can move on to the next step toward optimizing your performance.

CHAPTER TWO

Trading Inherited Weaknesses for Natural Strengths

Every human being has talents that are just waiting to be uncovered.

—Tom Rath

Beautiful things begin to happen when you start to know yourself and love yourself. Our change in mindset increases our ability to be the person we were meant to be. It gives us the power to choose the things we want to do and don't want to do. Subconsciously, we would often prefer to allow someone else to make the decision for us. That way, if things go awry, we can blame the circumstance or another person.

It's sad how many people spend years trying to mimic their parents or mentors. High school seniors choose universities based on their friends' acceptance letters. Without a mind transformation, young adults declare a college major according to the anticipated salary. Nearly fifty percent of students enter college undeclared, and seventy-five percent change their major at least once in their four- or five-year adventure.[12]

The confusion isn't limited to our late teens and early twenties. Most of us don't know what we want to be when we grow up because we don't know ourselves. Without a focus on our passion, we drift through life aimlessly, never excited about anything.

Social media doesn't help. We see what excites others and stop looking for what makes our own hearts beat faster. And so much of what we see is really just a façade. Still, we grab hold of someone else's hand-me-down dreams. With the world at our fingertips, we have a number of choices. If we don't have a firm grasp on who we are and what we want, we'll keep choosing the next exciting thing we see, and we won't get anywhere.

Fortunately, as we become more mentally fit and begin to know ourselves, we'll start to embrace our uniqueness and move away from struggling to act and live like those we admire. No longer will we try to be someone else. We will be able to leave the depression brought on by envy because we'll know ourselves and love ourselves.

Stop Chasing Your Weakness

Travis Ramsey says, "You can have and do anything you want. You just can't have and do everything." This means it's important to decide how we want to spend our time. When you look back over the past week, month, or year, what things have you done that made you feel accomplished? What things were most important? If you could have only one thing in your life, what would you choose? Which activities do you want to prioritize? What do you do best, and how can you best use your natural strength?

Sadly, many people don't believe they have any natural strengths. These folks just settle for mediocre living and spend the biggest portion of their time feeling stuck. Others strive after everything, so they never focus on the one thing they naturally do well. I call it a race to mediocrity. When we settle for the first thing we do adequately and don't move into the areas where we naturally excel, we miss the joy and contentment living and working in our natural strengths brings.

> You can have and do anything you want. You just can't have and do everything.
> –Travis Ramsey

I believe everyone has inherent natural abilities, and many scientists and experts agree. Discovering these natural strengths is imperative to truly knowing yourself. Julia Waller from Strategic Coach took me through a powerful exercise that helped me immensely. They had me ask about a dozen people what they believed my natural strengths were. This simple act was a huge key in discovering the real me. Many of the things my friends listed were things I took for granted. We assume everyone can do the things we do well because they're so easy for us.

Donald Clifton, the father of the CliftonStrengths® assessment, said:

> There is one sure way to identify your greatest potential for strength: Step back and watch yourself for a while. Try an activity and see how quickly you pick it up, how quickly you skip steps in the learning, and add twists and kinks you haven't been taught yet. See whether you become

absorbed in the activity to such an extent you lose track of time. If none of these has happened after a couple of months, try another activity and watch another. Over time your dominant talents will reveal themselves, and you can start to refine them into a powerful strength.

Donald Clifton

Unfortunately, if you've spent decades developing your weaknesses, you might not recognize your need to keep searching.

When our identity is lost in those around us, it's easy to miss our dominant talents; however, our new mindset means it's time to make certain we're focused on our own strengths.

In addition to CliftonStrengths helping you find your talents, the Kolbe A™ Index can reveal your innate conative strengths. You can take an IQ test to determine your cognitive abilities, a DISC® assessment to help others understand your personality, or a PRINT® Survey to identify your motivators. But the Kolbe Index helps identify another set of natural abilities—traits you've had since you were born, like your innate talents.

Kathy Kolbe recognized that each person has a unique way of solving problems, and she developed a way to measure it. Some thrive when they can gather facts, others need to organize and systematize. You might get to the heart of the matter best by brainstorming or keeping everything stable, and just as many people need to have hands-on experience to get a project started.

When I started working with Strategic Coach, they encouraged me to dig deep into my natural strengths—something they call Unique Ability. At first, I hesitated. Did I really want to make a lifelong commitment to one area? It felt like it could be a life sentence. But it's not. I can change the way I use my Unique Ability any time I choose. What I'm doing now is just a stepping stone to what I'm doing next.

Before I started working with Julia, I worked in the area of my Unique Ability about thirty percent of the time. After her training and spending intentional time with my assistant Stacy Stuckey focusing on what I needed to do to be more productive, I was able to increase my time in my natural strengths to approximately eighty percent.

Prior to this revelation, I wrote what I thought was my Unique Ability on both sides of a card. One side represented my personal life, and the other, my professional. As I worked on knowing myself better and recognizing my Unique Ability, the differences on the two sides of my card began to fade. I discovered the natural strengths I use professionally are the same ones I use personally.

Discovering this intuitive strength is a process. It will take time, but not as much time as reaching excellence with your weaknesses. When my personal and professional strengths finally merged, it was powerful. The realization gave me the feeling of being one hundred percent myself.

Don't Share the Suck

As we end this chasing after weaknesses, it's also important to recognize that every now and then, what some people classify as a weakness could be your superpower. For instance, while ADHD often creates stumbling blocks in the formal learning process, studies have shown the so-called disorder is displayed in higher percentages among entrepreneurs,[13] and "when harnessed properly, the attributes afforded to those with ADHD can be enormous assets, particularly in the business world."[14]

Trading Inherited Weaknesses for Natural Strengths

Tragically, people in the United States seldom focus on strengths—not their own and not those of others. Rather, we focus on the suck. We use weaknesses as the basis for jokes and ignore the fact some weaknesses have admirable traits associated with them. Parents do it. Friends laugh through it. We focus on the things we aren't good at and use the phrase, "I'm just built that way," to shrug off these areas that seem to hold us back.

Due to the high level of focus we put on these shortages, we then spend exorbitant amounts of time and money attempting to get better. The shame associated with our limitations drives us to bow to the pressure.

Humans have massive adaptability. It's a gift allowing us to be mentally resilient and survive when life doesn't go according to plan. However, it also means we can perform well in areas outside our natural strengths, and we end up miserable.

For instance, many people wish they could play an instrument. So, they struggle through lessons. It's an admirable endeavor and great for your health. Learning to play an instrument builds positive neurons and strengthens every part of our central nervous system as we tap into both sides of our brain.[15] On the other hand, if we have only a basic talent for music, dedicating hours and hours of time to perfect the weakness steals precious minutes we can use to move toward excellence in a skill that comes as naturally as breathing.

> **Focusing on weaknesses sets us up for an average life with average joy and average pay at best.**

Embracing our natural strengths allows us to shake off the shame, whether it comes from within or from others. We become immune to the ridicule because we own the things we're good at and release the areas that cause us to strive for mediocrity. Focusing on weaknesses sets us up for an average life with average joy and average pay at best. Most of the world has settled for this mediocrity.

When you find you're unnecessarily holding on to jobs outside your natural strengths, it's important to ask why. Many women feel like the household tasks are their job regardless of the drain. Do we hold on to those tasks out of guilt, duty, identity, or something else? I really think it's because we don't truly love ourselves. Sometimes we hold on to those exhausting tasks to torture ourselves. When we love ourselves, we'll give ourselves permission to say no and delegate tasks outside our giftedness.

In a marriage, a lot of times, we want to make sure everyone in the household is carrying his or her load. We feel cheated if it seems like we're doing all the thankless jobs. Even when we can afford to pay someone to take care of those things outside our natural strengths, we may try to impose our opinion on the other person. We need to be aware of our feelings—know ourselves. If we're doing things outside our natural abilities, we need to find a way to delegate rather than pass on our own discontent.

That's not to say you won't ever do hard things or add hobbies, skills, or strengths to your life. Maybe you want to learn to surf, but you've never surfed a day in your life. You'll probably start out falling more than surfing. It may take you thousands of hours to get good at it. Like our instrument example earlier, if it's something you truly want to learn, you should do it. If it interests you, try it at least once. Don't miss out on something fun simply because it's not your strength. The experience feeds your neurons. The point is everything new you try should be your choice. We should avoid building weaknesses because we feel pressure from our parents, bosses, spouses, or friends.

Trading Inherited Weaknesses for Natural Strengths

Understanding your natural strengths and how they apply to your life frees you to be uniquely you. It also allows you to affirm others' natural strengths and encourage them to work in them. If you and your spouse have complementary strengths, and you allow each other to use them without interference, it can make home life run more smoothly. You'll obviously have some crossover, and occasionally you'll step into your spouse's role because of time constraints, illness, or life changes. Nevertheless, the freedom you both will feel because you get to contribute in the most natural way possible will create a little corner of Heaven in your home.

Why would we want the person we love to work outside their natural abilities? Shouldn't we help them find the peace and happiness available when they do what they do best? Sadly, that's not usually the case. It's because we want the people around us to be as miserable as we are—we want them to share the suck. Parents do it to children; bosses impose it upon employees. We don't mean to. Most of the time, we're not even aware of what we're doing. This makes it even more vital to be aware of our natural strengths and the natural strengths of our spouses, children, and coworkers.

Imagine what would happen if we led the way to stop sharing the suck. What would your household look like if you started watching for your children's natural strengths and encouraged them to improve them and work on them? Children as young as pre-teen will begin to display their natural strengths. Often when they're young, they're the traits that drive you crazy.

My assistant's daughter knows everything about everybody. Right now, it looks like she's nosy, and hearing the details of what everyone did all day can get annoying; however, those investigating skills will be valuable when she enters the job market. The same child loves math and lists. She wants her chores written so she knows what to do. While the average parent will tell her she doesn't need a piece of paper with "clean your room" written on it, a parent who recognizes natural strengths sees her need to have a system in place.

Recognizing natural strengths makes people feel seen and loved like they've never felt seen or heard before. It creates a connection, and people want more of it because it's not common.

How might the world change if every person who read these words refused to highlight the weaknesses of those around her? Consider the power we could give the next generation if we focused on strengths rather than the things people stumble over. And you'll be amazed at the power you create at work when you and your colleagues all focus on knowing themselves and their strengths.

Filling the Gaps

When I returned from Strategic Coach with the goal of working in my Unique Ability, I wanted my assistant, Stacy, and my entire tribe to have the freedom to work in her natural strengths as well. I had one fear. If I encouraged my entire team to focus on their natural strengths, how many gaps would I have? Would they be able to find someone else to do the work that didn't fall in their Unique Ability? I really wanted my tribe to be free to be their best selves, but I needed the company to continue to function smoothly.

As we began to disperse duties, I discovered I didn't need to worry about things not getting done. In fact, just the opposite happened. People embraced the permission to separate jobs based on natural strengths, and they had more bandwidth. Working within their natural strengths meant they could finish tasks two to five times faster than before. When something in their job description fell outside their natural strengths, they had the power to enlist someone whose natural strengths covered it. Everything got done, and it got done more efficiently.

Previously, I worked in any area of the company that needed assistance. For instance, I can hold my own when it comes to business administration and management, and I have done it for a long time. However, when I hired someone gifted in that area, I realized my skills paled in comparison. Just because I have the ability to do a job in my company doesn't mean I should.

I want to do more than just get by. I've discovered I'm great at brainstorming, innovation, bringing new ideas to the table, and getting things started. By embracing those natural strengths, I am more productive and have more energy.

As humans, we often find ourselves drawn to people who are like us. We gravitate toward folks in our age bracket or personality. But this means I could potentially have a full team of people with the same natural strengths as me. We wouldn't get much accomplished.

After I saw the success we had when everyone worked in their strengths, I began to use the Kolbe Index, PRINT, and CliftonStrengths assessments to direct my hiring. Now I ask, "What kind of person do we need to fill these holes?" Which ability, personality, or innate strengths will work here best?

Some will point out I have the luxury of a nice-sized team to fill in the gaps that fall outside my natural strengths. They will feel like they are trapped because they don't have a team of two hundred fifty. Granted, it makes it easier to find someone to do things outside my Unique Ability with such a great tribe, but everyone starts small. One of the reasons I have so many people in my tribe is because I gave myself and my team permission to work in their Unique Ability.

Plus, I have a much happier, more content group of folks in our tribe. People were thrilled when I handed off jobs to them. I discovered many of them had been watching me do some of those tasks, thinking, *Please let me do that.* What I agonized over for hours, members of my team completed in ten minutes. My direct reports love being able to come to me and say, "Mike, I'm just not good at that," knowing I will help them find someone to do that part of the project.

You will make more money, be more satisfied, and have the ability to add to your team sooner if you stay within your Unique Ability as much as possible. You'll still need to sometimes do the difficult stuff, but, honestly, none of us will ever be able to work in our natural strengths one hundred percent of the time. However, if we stay in our lane eighty or ninety percent of the time, those times we work outside our strengths become the spice of life. They keep things interesting. It's okay to take the garbage out once in a while, you just don't want to do it every moment of every day.

Finding Balance

When we know and love ourselves, we can effectively take control of our days. Because we perform more efficiently, it will feel like we have extra hours. But will we squander them or spend them wisely?

Working in our natural strengths and remaining mentally fit allows us to be the CEO of our lives. This means we have the power to actively shape our destiny and make intentional choices. We get to take charge of our self-care, our relationships, and our boundaries.

For example, when we have business planning meetings, I attend. It's my business, and I want my fingerprints to be all over it. On the other hand, I dread the meetings. They're just not in my wheelhouse. So, I've taken control of the situation.

Long before the meeting, I informed someone with different natural strengths he was going to be in charge. I would be there to innovate and make sure we stayed true to the vision of the community, but my colleague would take the group into the deep dive. We parsed out our duties in the meeting ahead of time. This allowed us to get in there with no false expectations.

Understanding my natural strengths has brought balance to our company. It's helped me adapt my leadership style. Some things have been delegated to my assistant. My colleague has taken on some of the other tasks. When someone approaches me about something one of them has taken leadership on, I refer them to the person in charge rather than field the question myself. Sometimes the person comes to me because he or she assumes I have a final say or will make adjustments to the projects after these other leaders make a decision, so they want to have the discussion with me first. But since I've discovered how to balance the natural strengths of the company, I trust my companions in leadership to do what they do well, and I stay out of it. We want every person to work in the area where they'll shine and help them avoid the work they'll be terrible at.

We also have to balance our mindsets. Well-meaning parents and grandparents pass down outdated traditions—ideas about how families should operate or the way you should work. There's often guilt associated with pursuing careers outside the family's norm or using your natural strengths in non-traditional ways. It's important to shed the inherited bad advice while keeping the customs that bring you peace and inspire good memories.

When you combine mental fitness and resilience with natural strengths, you become a formidable figure. Because you know yourself, you can love yourself. People who love themselves do what they can to stay healthy—physically, mentally, and emotionally.

I am a recovering workaholic. After working on myself, I do much better at balancing my life most of the time. Balance means your personal life and your professional life each get your intentional attention. True balance starts with transforming ourselves. You give yourself permission to spend as much time building yourself as you do building relationships. It means you love yourself enough to be confident, but you love others enough to avoid arrogance.

Scheduling days off, enjoying the outdoors, and spending quality time with our families are just as important as eating right and getting some exercise. When you know yourself, you'll sense when you need extra sleep or coffee with a friend. A balanced life gives you permission to take time for yourself without feeling guilty.

The way we apply this philosophy of balance to ourselves, our close relationships, and our work tribe will dictate our performance at work. When we take care of ourselves and our families, we can appropriately focus on our careers and enjoy Heaven on Earth both personally and professionally.

CHAPTER THREE

Setting Yourself Up for Success: Defining Your Mission, Vision, and Values

We become what we think about most of the time.
—Earl Nightengale

After you identify and begin to work in your natural strengths, you'll have more clarity regarding where you want to be in one, five, or ten years. You'll be able to lay out a plan to use those strengths to reach your goal, and because you know yourself, you'll understand what drives you to reach that target. It's what we call our mission, vision, and values.

When you know and love yourself, the things you believe are most important in your life consistently float to the top. Few ever consider their individual core values. We tend to grab hold of the values of people or organizations around us. However, if we examine the statements we resonate with, we can begin to identify our own. Even without writing them down or formally stating them, the more intimately we know ourselves, the more we see these uncompromising standards we carry deep within us.

Being aware of your values and life mission can help you succeed in many areas. Dating based on values and what you want for your future gives you an advantage if you're looking for someone to spend the rest of your life with. Knowing yourself in this vital place in the pyramid will give you direction as you select courses, college, or continuing education. It will lead you to your ideal career or send you into the perfect entrepreneurship.

Setting your mission, vision, and values is an extension of loving yourself. Knowing why you pursue your mission and what the future of your mission looks like encourages you to foster healthy collaborations rather than seeking change for change's sake. Plus, these collaborations become an active gathering of a tribe of people who align with your personal and professional mission, vision, and values. You gain confidence and your mental fitness increases.

Identifying Your Values

At L&H, we have four values core to our existence. The first is Do The Right Thing. We want to demonstrate integrity in every avenue of our business. Our character is every bit as important to us as the quality of our work.

Second, we want to Make an Impact. Every project has an aspect of "How can we use this to make the community better?" Our innovations begin with thinking about the people whose lives will be enhanced because we acted.

Setting Yourself Up for Success: Defining Your Mission, Vision, and Values

L&H Industrial has set our third value as Lead by Example. We expect our team to consistently show respect, always seek knowledge, continually pursue excellence, and never stop demonstrating how much we value growth. When we live this and people see our success, they'll want to mirror what we do.

Finally, but perhaps most importantly, we Love People. You're right. This is not your typical business value. In fact, we define this goal as a disruption of the industry. After reading Viktor Frankl's *Man's Search for Meaning*, I pondered his words for a good while. Frankl helped me realize love is the most important thing. If we can love ourselves and others well, we probably have mental fitness and mental resilience, know our natural strengths, and have our values right. We can't really love fully until we have all the rest together.

At L&H, we want our deep level of care, grace, honesty, and compassion for ourselves, our customers, our partners, and even our competitors to set us apart. And if we do it right, this value will become a part of Lead By Example. We can sum up our core values in four simple words: Integrity, Impact, Inspiration, and Love.

Values are authentic statements you can embrace and live out.

Knowing your values is essential to the success of your company. In fact, as an individual, speaking your core values aloud and clearly identifying them can be tremendously empowering. It will definitely put you a step ahead of other candidates interviewing for the position you want.

Unfortunately, you can't merely wish values into existence. They can't be aspirational. You need authentic statements you can embrace and live out. Many companies fake it till they make it, but it's nearly impossible to succeed in pretend mode. Obviously, some businesses have grown without a clear mission, vision, and values. However, true mental fitness means we know who we are and what we stand for. This clarity allows us to perform more efficiently. It also sets the stage for those who work with us. They have a better idea of what to expect from us. And if they have a strong understanding of their own values, it allows everyone to foresee problems and conflicts.

The set of values I listed above has morphed over the years. We began with a value of Safety First, which is now integrated into Do the Right Thing. Some might have thought it aspirational at the time because our company faced accident after accident, one so tragic I knew I could never let anything of that magnitude happen again. So, even though we weren't living it when we wrote it, the value of Safety First resonated deep within my soul. It was something I couldn't quit thinking about. I didn't just hope someday our company could be a safe place to work; I was determined to make L&H a leader in industrial safety.

We also began with the value of being world-class. Though this has been absorbed into Do Things the Right Way and Lead by Example, at the time, we fell way short. However, as soon as we made the decision to embrace these new values, we changed the way we operated. Action moves your values out of the realm of aspirational into reality.

Gino Wickham and his Entrepreneurial Operating System (EOS)® stress the importance of using core values as the basis to hire, fire, reward, and recognize. To carry out the things we felt were most important, we had to let go of people according to the values we set. I think we implemented our values a bit too slowly, but we cared about the people on our team and hated to hurt them; however, employees whose values don't align with the company will be hurt regardless.

Setting Yourself Up for Success: Defining Your Mission, Vision, and Values

The discomfort the misalignment brings can be overwhelming to the entire tribe. We should have weighed the immense pain caused by keeping people whose values were out of sync against the temporary pain of letting those people go and moved more quickly.

While employees' values might not mesh one hundred percent with the values of the company, with leaders, there can be no compromise. Mismatches just won't work. Lying to yourself, your employees, or your customers at any level isn't helpful. And let's face it, the truth is just more interesting. People can sense candor. Even when it's messy, the people in your life—professionally and personally—will always prefer honesty.

Many people water down the truth or try to make it more pleasant. They believe the old movie quote, "You can't handle the truth." But look at the number of people who don't trust the government because the facts get twisted and statistics become filtered so politicians can prove their point. I've discovered most people can handle the truth; they can't handle being lied to.

One of my personal core values is Freedom. While love tops my individual list, I believe the freedoms we have in the United States are our second most important value. Patrick Henry and I have a like-minded attitude: "Give me liberty or give me death." I've traveled the world, and each country I visit makes me appreciate the freedom we have in this country even more. I've not found another place with as much freedom as we enjoy.

This value of freedom includes giving myself the freedom to be me. While love keeps me from infringing on others' freedoms with my own, keeping the realization I am free to be myself in my consciousness helps form my Heaven on Earth.

When you embrace strong values, you can own what's most important to you. When someone cuts you off in traffic, and it wrecks your morning, your values can help you understand why you resort to anger. Do your emotions reflect your value of minutes? Are those few seconds they stole really worth ruining your day? Or are you angry because you value respect and you feel as though they disrespected you? Understanding your values and how they trigger your emotions can help transform your mind and give you control over those feelings that seem to bring out the worst in you.

Embracing your values also empowers you to choose which relationships you will invest in. Many times, people get stuck because they're afraid of alienating friends or family. Placing a high importance on your values, and developing relationships based on those criteria takes the pressure off when we're spending less time with people we've known for years.

Without values, fear drives us, and we end up stranded. We feel as though we're stuck in quicksand. Unfortunately, we're more like ships on the sea. It's impossible to stay put. Even with a great anchor, when the storms come, the waves lift the boat beyond the capabilities of the sea weight and move the craft away from its point of reference. We can't remain static. Without values to steer us, we're like ships without a rudder.

Crafting a Compelling Vision

I believe vision is perpetually imagining how your ideal future could look and becoming very intentional about getting there. I learn from my past and use that knowledge to picture an excitingly remarkable future. Your vision statement puts words to your why. Why do you want to do what

Setting Yourself Up for Success: Defining Your Mission, Vision, and Values

you want to do? What is your purpose? Who do you want to impact? Understanding your natural strengths and core values allows you to define and refine your vision.

My own vision is perpetual improvement for the good of mankind, love, and freedom. Knowing this sets me on a path to continually look for ways to have a positive impact on my community as well as our industry. My vision inspired me to help found the Wyoming Innovative Entrepreneurs group to grow and diversify our state's advanced manufacturing, as well as serve on a variety of state and local committees and boards designed to improve the local economy.

The vision of L&H is to transform the future by transforming machines. To our customers, we're the go-to place for heavy machinery parts and repair, and we want to be bigger. Transforming machines is easy, but how can we use those changes to transform the future?

The best vision statements are very clear and cause others to get excited about them as well. Look at your natural strengths and core values. How can you meld the two to create a better future for yourself, your family, and your community? Does the answer excite you? Will it excite others who share your values? If not, keep looking. When you find a vision statement that's a good fit, you'll feel something inside stir. Your vision statement will inspire you to take action.

Forging a Mountain-Moving Mission

While your vision should be future-focused, your mission will include your plan to make your vision true starting today. It forces us to answer a few questions. Where do you want your vision to happen? What can I do today to bring my vision closer to reality? And how can I implement my who, what, when, where, and why?

Peter Diamandis stresses the need to find our Massive Transformative Purpose. I searched for mine for years, and finally, I came to realize my personal MTP, my mission, is To Innovate Energy. I love looking for affordable and sustainable ways to power the planet and the humans on it. This passion to innovate energy will help me see my vision come to fruition. Innovating energy sources will produce the momentum to perpetually improve the planet for the good of everyone around me.

Most people don't realize, however, that coal, oil, gas, solar, water, wind, and nuclear energy sources are just the beginning. As I mentioned earlier, these represent mere tools in the hands of the true power plants. Human energy holds the keys to the most important kind of power.

My MTP is To Innovate Energy.

One of the reasons I love the L&H tribe is their ability to create great energy. Not energy to power your lights, but an energy that lifts others. They understand how to harness their energy to get the job done more efficiently and cost-effectively while still keeping it as safe as humanly possible. Our growth and our ability to attract and retain the best employees in the industry are limited only by the amount of energy produced by our team, and they've created a relatively limitless supply. They understand personal energy is the gold mine.

The L&H tribe helps me carry out my personal mission as we live out the mission of the company: to move the industry forward by designing, manufacturing, and maintaining the biggest machines on Earth. The energy they create as they practice their natural strengths is phenomenal. They live out the vision and mission using the manufacturing of big machine parts to transform the future.

Bigger Than You Might Imagine

Many organizations and individuals set visions and missions way beyond what others think possible. To someone who feels limited by their own mindset, your mission and vision may seem lofty and unattainable. And honestly, if you never see your vision fulfilled, you needn't feel bad. When you chase an ambitious vision, you'll create tremendous ripples along the way. The impact of the journey will be enough.

On the other hand, sometimes our mission and vision will be something we can't accomplish entirely on our own. We need strong collaborations. Those healthy relationships you built while you were shoring up your foundation will become invaluable as you embark on a vision meant to change the future for everyone around you. Your mission, vision, and values will give you direction, and after you have a strong purpose and plan, it's time to plant your feet at the top of the pyramid.

CHAPTER FOUR

Accomplishing More in Less Time: The Art of Flow

> *Mindset impacts emotion, which alters biology,*
> *which increases performance.*
> *Thus, it seemed, by tinkering with mindset...*
> *one could significantly enhance performance.*
>
> —Steven Kotler

Distractions surround us. Even alone in a quiet room, most of us have the ding of a notification occasionally. The average person checks their phone every twelve minutes and looks at it approximately one hundred fifty times every day. Add meetings, e-mails, task-switching, thinking about the argument you had an hour ago, and boredom, and you can begin to see how easily we lose valuable time for productivity.

Accomplishing More in Less Time: The Art of Flow

Fortunately, late in the last century, psychologists and scientists began looking at high-performing individuals to find out how they achieved at such a consistent rate. Scientists discovered that while we can process between twenty and four hundred bits of information per second with our conscious mind, our subconscious mind is capable of processing more than four billion bits in the same time frame.

The professionals noticed this state of high achievement in athletes first. Sports professionals described it as effortless performance and becoming one with the sport. Everything they did felt right and easy. A runner in the zone will often not feel the pain associated with his last mile, and even though they outperform everyone else in their class, the feeling of being able to perform at their highest level outweighs the reward of winning.

It's a state that psychologist Mihály Csíkszentmihályi coined: flow. Some call it being in the zone, jazz musicians tell us they're playing in the pocket, and runners label the state a runner's high. Csíkszentmihályi described it as a state of optimal human performance. It's a peak where you tap into the subconscious so you can do and feel your best, and it's available to everyone.

Making the Pyramid Work for You

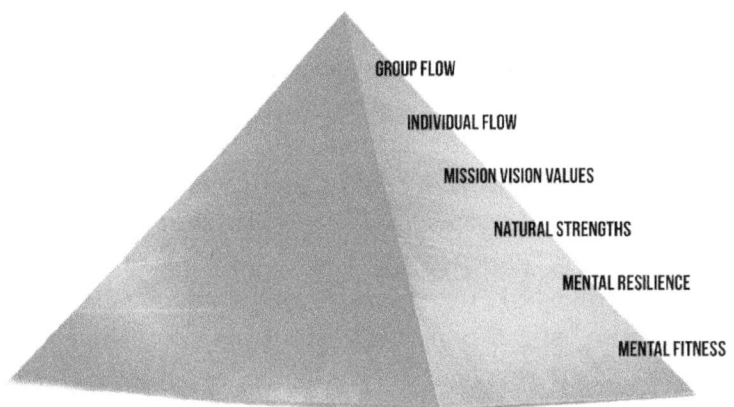

There at the top of the Performance Pyramid, you'll see flow. When I drop into this state of high productivity, I can accomplish the most good for myself and everyone around me. It seems almost spiritual. I become so in line with my nature that I can operate smoothly. Flow creates a euphoric state and feels rewarding. And while it rests there on top of the Pyramid, it begins at the bottom.

Getting into flow begins in the mind. And though it's not something we can completely control, we can create the perfect conditions for it. Step one is removing the distractions. Put your phone on silent and turn off email notifications. Tell your team you don't want to be disturbed for an hour. Some people crave distractions. They need the noise to cover the thoughts in their mind, but if this describes you, you might need to go back to transforming your mind. Often, we have to work through whatever causes us to rely on the noise. Whatever has the potential to take your mind away from the task at hand needs to be censored.

Accomplishing More in Less Time: The Art of Flow

Next, you'll want to make sure you're working in your natural strengths. While it might not be impossible to move into flow outside those innate talents, it's certainly not as productive, and I recommend using flow sparingly outside your Unique Ability. Athletes who fall into flow all move in the area of their greatest strength and give one hundred percent of their focus to the game.

Becoming totally absorbed in the moment is the third secret to getting into the zone. You give the task at hand your extreme focus. You often won't hear anything that doesn't pertain to your task. In athletes, it means mistakes and victories from past games have no influence over their current situation. There is no past nor future. In fact, you don't really have any sense of self.

One of the most difficult distractions to control is your thoughts, which proves the importance of the foundation of the pyramid. Loving yourself and knowing yourself are imperative to moving in flow. These qualities will help when your brain wants to jump to something else. Plus, the negative self-talk attacking many who attempt to focus will be minimal. We have the freedom to decide where we allocate our attention. Flow happens only when we make a conscious decision to concentrate every bit of our attention on what we're doing in that moment. You can't accomplish two cognitive things at one time. The few seconds you spend redirecting your thoughts when a notification goes off or someone walks into the room interrupts your flow and reduces your productivity.

Learning to be in the here and now will not only help you work in flow, but it also has the potential to strengthen relationships as you give your whole self to the time you spend with your spouse, children, and friends.

When your attention stays fixed on your mission and vision, and you stay true to your values, you'll find it easier to move into a place of increased productivity. In fact, time will seem to slow down as your ability to complete tasks faster increases. The shift in your brain waves and the neurochemicals it releases take you to a place of euphoria. Many people feel so good in flow that they try to stay there longer than they should. The extreme focus shortens the time it takes for you to reach mastery level in your natural strength, and you reach your optimal performance level. Steven Kotler believes productivity can be increased by five hundred percent when we work in flow.

If you have problems getting into flow and can't seem to recover, dropping back to the bottom of the pyramid can be helpful. Often, we'll discover our mindset shifted a bit or a trauma from our childhood we weren't aware of needs dealt with—like my water incident. Regardless of how well you've completed the Pyramid, a crisis is likely to hit you or your family, especially if the rest of your family hasn't had the privilege of meeting with a mental fitness coach or working the Pyramid.

By looking at your mental fitness and resilience, making sure you're still working in your natural strengths, and reviewing your mission, vision, and values, you can adjust where needed and work your way back into flow. Fortunately, the higher you get on the Pyramid and the more often you climb, the less often you'll fall into crisis. Plus, the more you work at it, the stronger the foundation becomes. You get it tamped down and well settled. Falling out of flow for long periods may just require periodic checks on how your current position fits with your strengths and values.

The bigger the foundation, the more accessible the higher levels, and the easier it is to construct your Heaven on Earth. Everything builds on reprogramming your thoughts, shedding the programming you've received from various other sources, and telling yourself you're worthy and you deserve to live in euphoria.

Getting Flow to Work for You

It would be handy if we could flip a switch and enter flow state. But understanding the stages and the need for every phase of the cycle can be almost as gratifying.

The first stage is the struggle or challenge phase. Many never get past this point because, as you may have guessed, it means you have to push yourself. You might feel frustrated as you overload your brain with information. The struggle phase offers one more reason we need mental fitness. The growth mindset we develop when we push our brains to create positive neurons and get rid of the negative ones will help get us through this stage. You don't want to burn yourself out with an excess of new processes, but without a challenge and some new information, your brain won't be pressed. It's a Goldilocks kind of moment. With just the right amount of stress, our brain releases chemicals to help tighten our focus.

After you've propelled yourself to the limit, it's time to move to the release stage. Though it sounds counterintuitive for flow, you need a break. A walk in the park or a catnap will work. Light physical activities like crafts or gardening also do the trick. Take ten to twenty minutes to allow the chemicals released in this stage to replace the stress chemicals and prepare us for what we've been waiting for: flow.

By returning to your original activity, your brain is now ready to dive in and show off her superpower. If you're mentally fit and prepared to truly focus, the self-critical part of your brain shuts off, and your cognitive and physical capabilities have the potential to explode. The release of a crazy combination of neurochemicals makes you feel like you can't fail. While we'd like to remain in this stage forever, we'll eventually have to move on. You use an enormous amount of energy while you're here. Granted, you'll get more done than normal, so the loss of energy won't hit as hard.

This brings us to the final stage: recovery. It's time to reward your brain, and perhaps your muscles, for all their hard work. Without this stage, flow will become more and more difficult. It's like attempting to start your car without any fuel. Flow empties your tank; recovery allows you to refill. Get some sleep, take a bath, do some cool-down exercises, or give yourself a nutritious treat and some water or a post-workout drink.

Most high performers struggle with recovery. They want to stay in flow because they feel so productive, and the chemical euphoria the brain creates calls to them. However, everyone needs to move into recovery. Our brains require the energy recovery creates so we can be prepared for our next session in flow.

Don't Make it Too Easy

Steven Kotler says, "To really achieve anything, you have to be able to tolerate and enjoy risk. It has to become a challenge to look forward to. In all fields, to make exceptional discoveries, you need risk—you're just never going to have a breakthrough without it." But let's face it; taking risks is scary.

Flow can be tough until you get accustomed to it. Some experts say you end up working five percent harder in flow. But because

> **To really achieve anything, you have to be able to tolerate and enjoy risk. - Steven Kotler**

I'm very cognizant of energy, I don't think we work harder; I believe we merely exert five percent more energy which causes us to work faster and more efficiently. However, part of the increased productivity will come because you won't be afraid to tackle challenges.

Challenge keeps life interesting, and it's an important part of the struggle phase. After we master one aspect of a craft, we want to move ahead and learn the next component. The average person gets bored doing something too easy. This explains why many people like to listen to audiobooks while they clean house or take their morning run. The physical activities offer no challenge, but even a good fiction book will stimulate our brains and force us to think from new perspectives.

This also means our natural abilities will be honed each time we use them. Boredom will invite us to push through to a higher level. We'll be challenged to try something new, and if we've learned the joy of working in our natural strengths, we'll be drawn to perfect another thing we do well.

You might wonder how you can move through the four stages of flow while you're on the job. Most managers won't see the value in a walk around the building or a long lunch to reward your brain. Developing industry leaders who understand the value of the Performance Pyramid is paramount. We have the power to bring joy to the workplace, retain employees, and give our team a desirable place to come each day; however, in order to have Heaven on Earth in the office or the shop, we need great conductors.

We Need Great Conductors

When sixty to one hundred twenty musicians get together, they need someone to keep them in sync. The greatest orchestras have a maestro who sets the tempo and the tenor of the movement. He leads the instrumentalists to create

Know Thyself, Love Thyself

magnificent swells as well as moments of silence the audience doesn't dare interrupt. Understanding the strengths and abilities of every violin player and percussionist, he uses the composer's score to draw out their talents and help them work as one to make the most beautiful music.

As a manager in a business striving to help their tribe reach flow, you have the opportunity to become just such a conductor. It's up to you to make sure each person on your team is willing to align with the company's mission, vision, and values, encourage them to have a transformational mindset and help them understand the importance of individual flow. If you watch those musicians in the orchestra, you'll see each one appears to be totally absorbed in the music. Their entire bodies feel the rhythm. Nothing exists in that moment other than their instrument, the notes on the page, and the maestro.

Conductors in other industries have the same obligation. These leaders provide the blueprint for the finished product, then they allow each person to play their instrument with their individual passions and techniques, creating harmony with everyone else on the team. Leaders need to allow everyone to have the space to be in flow and understand what others need to reach the state of highest performance.

I believe the Chicago Bulls of the 1990s played in flow. Each of those exceedingly talented men moved in the area of his greatest strength. They stayed completely focused—immersed in the moment. With the help of their coaches, they worked together seamlessly, taking the team to six championships in eight years and demonstrating the epitome of team flow.

Team flow is a bit more difficult to achieve than individual flow because of the variety of personalities and talents involved. If you're a member of the tribe, it's vital for you to

Accomplishing More in Less Time: The Art of Flow

learn how to harness the power of flow so you don't hold back your coworkers.

Managers who put team flow to work for them get an added benefit as it's fun to watch other people in flow. The efforts resemble a work of art, and the rewards of flow are exponential. For instance, when people don't feel forced to do a job, they're more likely to do it with joy. They do it faster, with higher quality, and they want to stay on the job past retirement age. The retention factor minimizes training, giving you even more time for production.

It takes a great leader to create group flow, and creating such a leader can happen accidentally or intentionally; however, the magic happens when the process becomes intentional. It's great if the person in charge has a title because authority and responsibility naturally accompany the position, but simply giving someone a position doesn't guarantee they will excel in a leadership position.

Sometimes these pacesetters rise up from within the organization. At L&H, we find them because we've intentionally allowed mentally fit and intelligent people to carry the titles. These men and women aren't afraid to give the up-and-coming managers the space to step up and use their natural strengths.

Other times we reach an exponential level of productivity due to several leaders combining their natural strengths. Because they know and love themselves, they don't need to compete. The most effective leaders don't care about their titles. They check their egos at the door and carry out a shared goal of helping every member of the tribe to excel at being their best self.

Intentionally choosing the right people with the appropriate natural talents for each position is key to group flow. If you continually wait for happy, accidental flow, it won't be sustainable or repeatable. Intentionality increases your odds of duplicating your productivity rate exponentially. Leaders will have to upskill, transfer, or replace the people who don't fit.

Team leaders who expect group flow watch for mentally fit people who have a mission, vision, and values aligned with the tribe. Additionally, these leaders create conditions for each individual in the tribe to drop into personal flow. It's not an easy task managing a group with the power of exponential productivity. Don't let the job intimidate you. And don't make the mistake of beating yourself up when it doesn't run perfectly. You can simply learn and adjust as you go. Knowing and practicing team flow will make you an extraordinary leader, and because it's such a beautiful thing to watch, you'll have customers begging you to take care of them.

Team flow isn't limited to businesses. Volunteer organizations and families can experience team flow, too. They simply need a leader willing to be the conductor. With a bit of practice, you can orchestrate flow and create Heaven on Earth for yourself as well as your tribe.

PART THREE
Practice

CHAPTER FIVE

Staying On Top

*The things you think about
determine the quality of your mind.
Your soul takes on the colour of your thoughts.*

—Marcus Aurelius

My experience with Travis was so effective, he became the on-call mental fitness coach for my entire family. Our family dynamic went through such a positive and dramatic transformation that I knew the tribe at L&H Industrial needed him.

We initially hired Travis to meet with each employee one-on-one for five sessions. However, we underestimated the power of an entire team of mentally fit gearheads. The results were so phenomenal that we extended Travis' reach to the employees' spouses and children.

Let me share how adding a mental fitness coach to our team affected my assistant, Stacy Stuckey:

My daughter was diagnosed with ADHD at the age of five. I always knew she had more energy than the other children, and her focus was never where it needed to be. Sadly, I carried that, blaming myself for her struggles.

When Travis met with my daughter, she opened up to him completely. After just a few sessions, he wanted to meet with me before he continued with my daughter. Travis helped me see I was so worried about my kids that I lost myself. He encouraged me to step back and look at the whole picture. I wanted to help them so much, but I couldn't help them until I helped myself.

Travis helped me see life in a completely different way. He helped to totally transform my thinking. I now believe each one of us is here to take control of ourselves. Yes, my daughter is highly energized, and my son shows signs of being similar. But when I looked from a more distant perspective, I could see they were kids reacting to their environment. My husband and I live a highly energized life. At the same time, we lead very successful lives, and we want to teach our children how to achieve.

I've learned my kids being different doesn't mean there is anything wrong with them. They will use their strengths to be very successful. We get one life to live. I now understand if I don't like something about my life, I have the power to change it. The key is putting in the work no one else wants to. I have to shine in my own way and help my kids do the same. Being me—who I really am—is loving myself. And I needed to learn to love myself before I could truly love anyone else.

The Most Valuable Type of Energy

Most of the trauma keeping people from being their best at work happens at home. Giving the whole family an opportunity to address those life-changing problems was a game-changer for our team. So, each employee and their family now have unlimited access to a world-class mental fitness coach.

The journey to flow is never-ending. A weightlifter can't reach his ideal size and then give up his daily training if he wants to maintain a high level of fitness. In the same way, we'll never be finished with our mental fitness regimen. It has to become a practice—a process we incorporate into our lives so deeply that the brain resets become automatic.

Travis has half a dozen different techniques he uses to help people discover their triggers. After we found the one that worked best for my personality, he taught me how to use it consistently. Enlisting the help of a mental fitness coach to train you to use the process that works best for you can be invaluable. The best coaches train you to work through the process until you can do it without their guidance. They help you work on your performance and focus on creating your Heaven on Earth rather than crisis.

It's not that you'll never ask for assistance again. Returning to your guide will be necessary from time to time. But the more you practice recognizing triggers and resetting, the less likely you are to explode.

Many who embark on this journey get held up because they think it will be too difficult. Change always feels hard. The people who hesitate focus on how burdensome the task will be. And while it does take a bit of work, it's so much easier on the other side. Mental fitness is merely feeding a new habit, like exercise or changing your diet—except giving yourself a new habit in the area of mental fitness means creating your own Heaven on Earth.

Of course, on the other side of the coin, when I explain to folks how easy life can be after they pursue mental fitness and natural strengths, many push it off as too good to be true. We're conditioned to believe life should be strenuous, so when someone like me or Travis comes along with tips on how to make life worthwhile, meaningful, and full of joy, they dismiss the idea before they try it. However, I counter-challenge with, "Why wouldn't you truly practice the principles you've read for at least sixty days? Test their merits. If you're a skeptic, maybe you'll be pleasantly surprised. What have you got to lose?"

Most people who reach the top of the pyramid don't even know they're there right away. It's just such a natural place to exist. And after they experience it at work, we see their epiphany. If this pyramid process gives me this much energy and productivity at work, why can't I incorporate it in my personal life? When we unlock the door to finding our most valuable resource—our energy—we discover the path to Heaven on Earth. By implementing these same principles in every aspect of your life—family, friends, volunteer organizations, as well as work—you realize life really can be incredible.

When you find yourself in crisis, you'll have to use mental resilience to recover. Fortunately, the more you practice mental fitness, staying in your natural strengths, following your mission, vision, and values, and getting into flow, the fewer crises you'll have.

As I mentioned, I'm an energy person. I look for ways to find more energy everywhere. So, I especially love this discovery of my personal sustainable energy source. In your work life, knowing yourself and loving yourself will allow you to work for more years if you want to. It gives you the confidence to create your own schedule and sets you up with the right team to pick up the slack when you want to back off a bit. Plus, you get to accomplish more in your lifetime.

Setting High Expectations

Your mind has more power than you might realize. I think we have the capability to live longer if we set our minds to it. If we believe we can live to two hundred rather than just seventy-five, we'll get much closer to two hundred. Better yet, our quality of life will improve simply because we feel like we have more control over how long we live. Expectations begin in the mind. If we control those expectations, we have more peace.

Think about the last time you waited for a friend at a restaurant. If they showed up ten minutes late but called to let you know, your frustration or worry level stayed low. On the other hand, those ten minutes seem like an hour when your expectations haven't been fulfilled.

> **Expectations begin in the mind. If we control those expectations, we have more peace.**

The same theory applies to our actions. When the average person is asked to do ten pushups, he struggles through to the end. And if he gets to the tenth pushup, and someone says, "You can do two more," it feels impossible.

When Tesla began producing Model 3 Sedans, Elon Musk ran the numbers and reported they needed to bring 5,000 cars a month off the assembly line in order to turn a profit. The feat seemed impossible. Nearly a year after he made the announcement, and even with massive streamlining, the two lines in Fremont, California, still had no way to keep up with that kind of goal.

With investors breathing down his neck, Tesla's CEO knew he had to get creative. A new building would take months, if not years, to complete. He needed a third line now.

While others would have accepted defeat, Musk did something no car manufacturer had done before—he secured a building permit to set up a massive white tent in the parking lot and set up a third assembly line to meet his goal. In a mere two weeks, they poured concrete and built the entire assembly line out of warehouse scraps. Less than a month later, the first Model 3 rolled off the new line. Musk set his sights high and didn't allow negativity to deter him.

When we begin with high expectations and a transformed mind, our natural abilities can take us to tremendous heights. Flow will increase our productivity, and setting lofty goals will help us reach our potential, a potential which we unfortunately keep a tight rein on.

Recognizing our expectations can also minimize friction in relationships and our lives. Much of our external and internal friction comes from unfulfilled expectations. If you help a friend move with the expectation he or she will help you when you move, and the friend opts not to help, you feel cheated or betrayed. However, if you think about it, the friend didn't let you down. Unless we voice our expectations before the trade-off begins, our friend has no obligation. Our frustration and disappointment actually stem from a lack of communication.

Mentally preparing ourselves and others for the situation means everyone handles it better. Beginning a difficult conversation with the phrase, "We need to talk, but I'm afraid this is going to be awkward and cause tension," makes the discussion much less tense and awkward.

Learning to manage expectations allows us to better handle those times when we're caught off guard and builds our mental resilience. We find we can be present in the moment and enjoy what is happening rather than focusing on what should have happened.

Quality of Life vs. Quantity of Life

Though I mentioned having a live-to-two-hundred mindset, if you're not enjoying life, the thought of living past eighty might be too much to handle. I think folks more commonly wonder why anyone would want to live for more than seventy-five years. A long life for those people feels like that race to mediocrity—it's a futile existence. Money won't fix it. Strong relationships might make it a little better. But the only road to a meaningful life is found in mental fitness. Without knowing yourself and loving yourself, the quantity of years is meaningless. Developing a refreshed mindset along with knowing your natural strengths and core values is the first step to a quality life.

> **External trappings, problems, and miseries life throws our way don't have to dictate the quality of our lives.**

If you haven't figured it out yet, I want to remind you—you have an enormous amount of control over your life. External trappings, problems, and the miseries life throws our way don't have to dictate the quality of our lives.

Even those in the most miserable circumstances have chosen to have a positive mindset. Viktor Frankl lived in a concentration camp for four years and watched his family be incinerated; still, he chose to have an internal quality of life. Mother Teresa lived in poverty among lepers. Still, her life exuded peace. After a year in Ravensbruck concentration camp, Corrie ten Boom went on to live to age ninety-one, creating rehabilitation centers for survivors of concentration camps, including those who helped the Germans.

A true quality life means taking care of the little things before they get to be big things. It's like going to the doctor for regular checkups instead of waiting until after you have a heart attack or stroke. There are so many places we can turn to for help: the assessments I mentioned, getting a coach who will walk with you as you dig through your past, as well as classes, podcasts, and books to give you more knowledge and power.

Looking into your past can be messy, and developing this new mindset is a process, not a date on a calendar. We have to learn to become comfortable with the uncomfortable and choose to face the truth with courage.

A quality life means adding beauty and wisdom to the continuum of your years. We'll find contradictory statements can exist on our continuum simultaneously. Rather than saying, "This world is beautiful, and I know many wonderful people, but . . ." we realize the world is beautiful, and there are many amazing people in it, AND some people aren't nice. Sometimes the beautiful world is full of destruction. Life and death both exist. The latter doesn't make the former untrue. By expanding our understanding of what can be true, we enlarge our capacity for a quality life.

Adopting this mindset and accepting the friction these contradictions bring allows us to grow and expand. You find you can be both scared and excited. You can love someone and not like their behavior. You develop stronger courage because you understand courage isn't the absence of fear. It's moving ahead despite fear.

This entire mindset has become the culture of L&H Industrial. We want our workplace to add to the quality of the lives of our tribe members. While other companies lose employees who get tired of certain aspects of their job or feel like there's some other portion they'd like to focus on more heavily, L&H expects individuals to let us know when they need to shed some of their duties or take on something new.

Building your Pyramid establishes a quality life. It creates a type of energy more valuable than any fossil fuel or green electricity. Practicing the life found in the Pyramid maximizes your ability to create Heaven on Earth.

You get to live your best life working in your natural strengths. Your self-worth increases because your transformed mind allows you to live out your values. And a pleasant by-product of climbing the Pyramid is increased revenue.

Crafting Your Own Heaven on Earth

Travis' coaching taught me the art of introspection. I can see myself clearly now—I look at who I am with eyes wide open. I know myself.

He also helped my family learn how to resolve issues and preemptively use our unique personalities to diffuse the situations causing life's complexities. My journey to Heaven on Earth unfolded with Travis' teaching. I realized it was more than simply achieving mental and emotional equilibrium. To create a true Heaven on Earth, I had to consciously attract the right kind of people and repel those who didn't align with my mission, vision, and values. I liken it to developing a personal immune system for maintaining my mental health and well-being.

When I attended the "40 Years of Zen" retreat with my wife, I had no idea the impact would continue to spread so many years later. Each phase of the development of what we now call Honestly Better Mental Fitness far exceeded my expectations. From the Zoom calls we implemented with our grown children to bringing Travis to the L&H facility for in-person visits with our tribe, the benefits of focusing on mental fitness and helping the people we live and work with to know and love themselves are immeasurable.

That's why we've created resources to bring others on this trek with us. Our YouTube channel hosts the archives of our *Honestly Better Mental Fitness* videos. You'll get to meet me in person and hear firsthand from Travis Ramsey as he helps the L&H team find the path to knowing and loving themselves. Look for us at YouTube.com/@honestlybettermentalfitness.

Additionally, the ever-expanding HonestlyBetterFitness.com website includes podcast episodes as well as a link to the "Mental Fitness Scorecard." The scorecard gives detailed explanations of the various stages of mental fitness development as well as your ability to identify your natural strengths and your likelihood of working in flow. On a scale of one through twelve, if you're willing to be honest with yourself, you can see the places you want to improve upon or get help with. We encourage you to take ten minutes to discover where you are on your own mental fitness journey.

Our family's story is a testament to the power of building mental fitness. From handling crises to enhancing personal performance and manifesting destinies, Travis' coaching made a monumental difference. He didn't just solve problems; he empowered us to become our own problem-solvers, to create environments where each of us could thrive and resonate with our deepest values and aspirations. We have become a collective of individuals who understand the significance of mental health, have learned to navigate life with resilience and grace, and are committed to creating our individual and collective Heavens on Earth. This journey has not only changed our lives, it has set a foundation for generations to come.

We invite you to link your journey to ours. Travel with us as we know ourselves better every day, love ourselves and each other deeper and stronger in each moment, and create a little piece of Heaven right here on Earth.

Endnotes

1 "The Law of Mirroring: What You See in Others Is Your Own Reflection," Exploring Your Mind, December 4, 2021, https://exploringyourmind.com/mirror-law-what-you-see-in-others-is-your-own-reflection/.

2 Perrin Elisha, "Can You Love Someone Else When You Don't Love Yourself?," Relationship Help, June 5, 2019, https://www.relationshipsrewired.com/blog/can-you-love-someone-else-when-you-don-t-love-yourself.

3 Hannah S. Packiam, "Food for Thought: How Negative Thinking Impacts Our Life & Health," Northeast Georgia Physicians Group, July 26, 2023, https://www.ngpg.org/food-for-thought-how-negative-thinking-impacts-our-life-health.

Endnotes

4 Courtney E. Ackerman, "What Is Neuroplasticity? A Psychologist Explains [+14 Tools]," PositivePsychology.com, October 13, 2023, https://positivepsychology.com/neuroplasticity.

5 Diana Rangaves, "The Relationship between Neuroplasticity and Positive Thinking," Re-origin, December 6, 2023, https://www.re-origin.com/articles/neuroplasticity-and-positive-thinking.

6 Kendra Cherry, "How Brain Neurons Change over Time from Life Experience," Verywell Mind, November 8, 2022, https://www.verywellmind.com/what-is-brain-plasticity-2794886.

7 "Physiology," Encyclopædia Britannica, accessed February 2, 2024, https://www.britannica.com/science/information-theory/Physiology.

8 "The Law of Mirroring: What You See in Others Is Your Own Reflection," Exploring Your Mind, December 4, 2021, https://exploringyourmind.com/mirror-law-what-you-see-in-others-is-your-own-reflection/.

9 Douglas LaBier, "Why Positive Relationships Are Needed for Emotional Health," Psychology Today, September 26, 2014, https://www.psychologytoday.com/us/blog/the-new-resilience/201409/why-positive-relationships-are-needed-emotional-health.

10 "10 Healthy Addictions That Won't Harm You," MPower Wellness, October 8, 2023, https://mpowerwellness.com/healthy-addictions/.

11 Jarlo Ilano, "Three Ways to Build Resilience for When Things Go Wrong," GMB Fitness, August 10, 2023, https://gmb.io/resilience/.

12 Kim-Ling Sun, "What Does It Mean to Be Undeclared?," BestColleges.com, August 23, 2022,

https://www.bestcolleges.com/blog/what-does-undeclared-mean/.

13   Nicos Nicolaou et al., "A Polymorphism Associated with Entrepreneurship: Evidence from Dopamine Receptor Candidate Genes - Small Business Economics," SpringerLink, December 16, 2010, https://link.springer.com/article/10.1007/s11187-010-9308-1.

14   Zachariah Booker, "Council Post: ADHD and Entrepreneurship: Helping Innovators Achieve Success," Forbes, January 9, 2023, https://www.forbes.com/sites/forbesbusinesscouncil/2023/01/06/adhd-and-entrepreneurship-helping-innovators-achieve-success/.

15   Sally Sapega, "Playing an Instrument: Better for Your Brain than Just Listening," Penn Medicine, January 30, 2017, https://www.pennmedicine.org/news/news-blog/2017/january/playing-an-instrument-better-for-your-brain-than-just-listening.

About the Author

Mike Wandler leads L&H Industrial's business strategy in building the blueprint for our future. With his deep experience in the company and immense business knowledge, Mike is instrumental in identifying new market opportunities. His inspiration for technology is what drives L&H's state-of-the-art machines, software, and innovation.

After achieving a bachelor's of business management from Kennedy Western and graduating from Harvards Business Schools Owner/President management program, Mike began his career at L&H Industrial as a laborer and machinist, eventually becoming the machine shop supervisor

About the Author

before becoming vice president of the company. He began leading the company as president in 2000 and was driven to improve L&H's capabilities, facilities, tools, processes, work culture, and opportunities. Over the years he has led a series of transformational initiatives that have re-defined how we do business.

Mike values love, freedom, mental and physical fitness, energy, and flow. He and his wife, Jerri, enjoy spending time with their seven adult children and twelve grandchildren.

Connect with Mike at
HonestlyBetterFitness.com/Contact

CONNECT WITH MIKE

Follow him on LinkedIn today.

Innovatewy.com/about

BETTER MENTAL FITNESS FOR BETTER RELATIONSHIPS

Podcast

Balancing a career, family, stress and many other factors can affect mental health. Learn how to improve your mental fitness for a happier stress-free life.

HonestlyBetterFitness.com

L&H Industrial is a leader in technology innovations, custom manufacturing, and comprehensive services for heavy industrial machinery used in heavy industries across the globe.

LNH.net

THIS BOOK IS PROTECTED INTELLECTUAL PROPERTY

The author of this book values Intellectual Property. The book you just read is protected by Instant IP™, a proprietary process, which integrates blockchain technology giving Intellectual Property "Global Protection." By creating a "Time-Stamped" smart contract that can never be tampered with or changed, we establish "First Use" that tracks back to the author.

Instant IP™ functions much like a Pre-Patent™ since it provides an immutable "First Use" of the Intellectual Property. This is achieved through our proprietary process of leveraging blockchain technology and smart contracts. As a result, proving "First Use" is simple through a global and verifiable smart contract. By protecting intellectual property with blockchain technology and smart contracts, we establish a "First to File" event.

Protected by Instant IP™

LEARN MORE AT INSTANTIP.TODAY

www.ingramcontent.com/pod-product-compliance
Lightning Source LLC
Chambersburg PA
CBHW052149070526
44585CB00017B/2046